For little ones everywhere

First Chronicle Books edition published in 2006.

Book design by Paul Rand.
Jacket flaps and copyright page typeset in ITC American Typewriter.
Manufactured in China.

Library of Congress Cataloging-in-Publication Data
    Rand, Ann.
        Little 1 / by Ann & Paul Rand.
            p. cm.
        Summary: Lonely number one is rejected by all the digits
        playing happily in their own groups, but with a friendly
        hoop as a zero they become the number ten.
        ISBN-13: 978-0-8118-5004-9 / ISBN-10: 0-8118-5004-8
        [1. Addition—Fiction. 2. Stories in rhyme. 3. Counting.]
        I. Title: Little one. II. Rand, Paul. 1914- III. Title.
        PZ8.3.R15Li 2005
        E—dc22
                        2004023259

Distributed in Canada by Raincoast Books
9050 Shaughnessy Street
Vancouver, British Columbia V6P E5

10 9 8 7 6 5 4 3 2 1

Chronicle Books LLC
85 Second Street
San Francisco, California 94105

www.chroniclebooks.com

Little 1

by Ann & Paul Rand

chronicle books · san francisco

Little 1 looked like a stick.
From the front he was medium thick,
but from the side he was so thin
he could have been
a line.

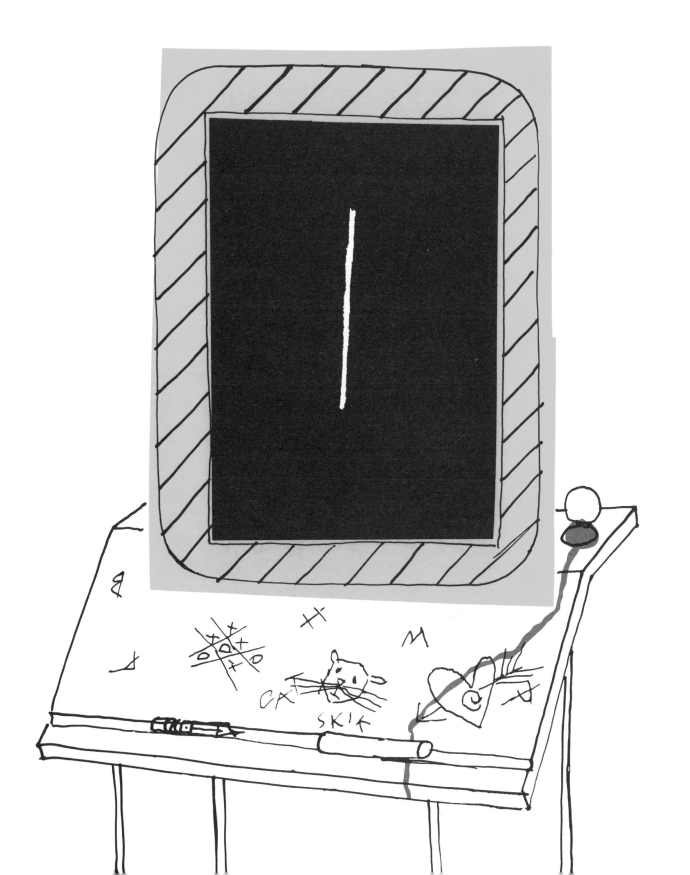

Little 1 had very small feet
and a little red hat
that sat on the tip of his head.
He could hop and skip and spin,
but he never had much fun
because he was only 1.

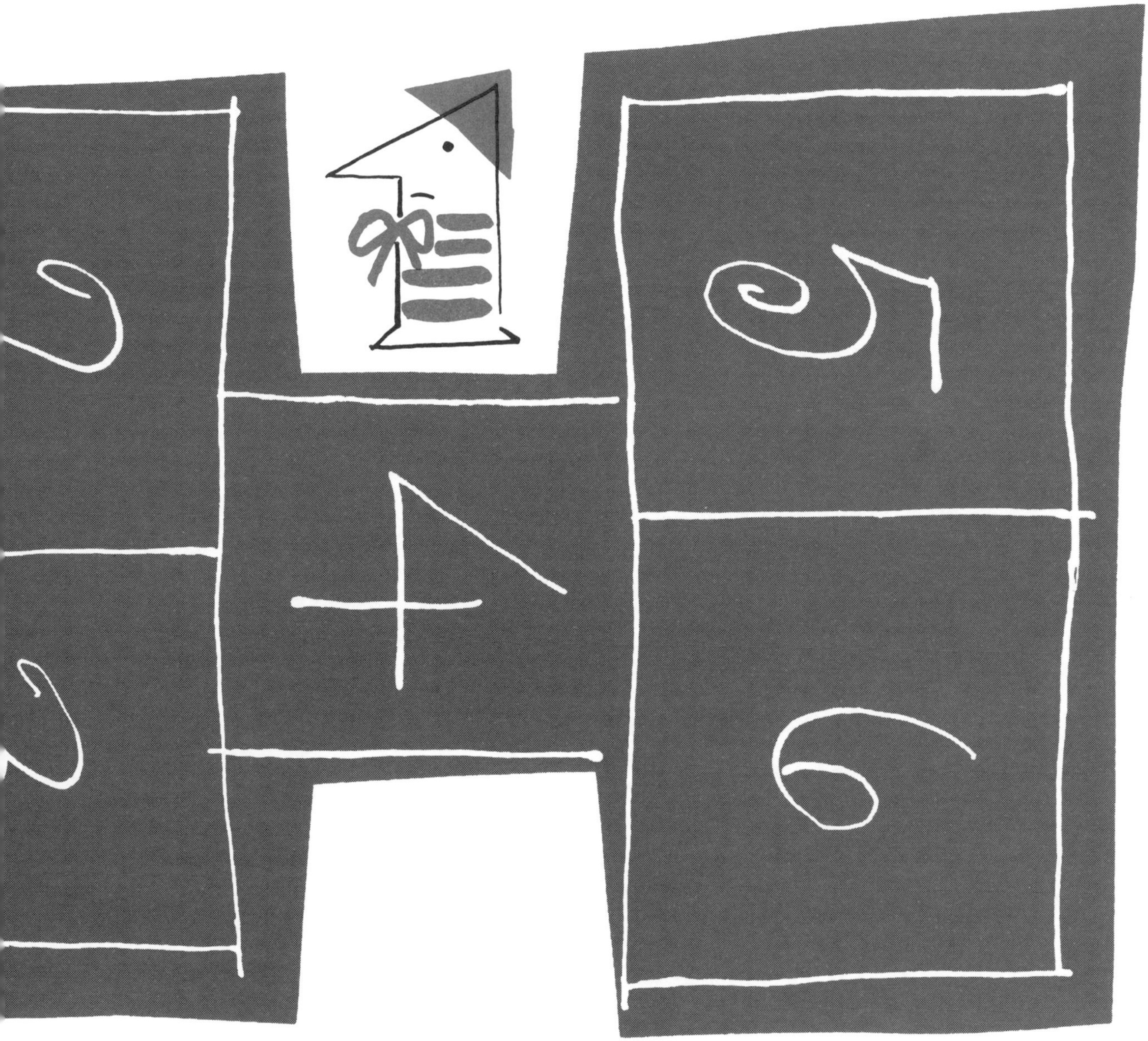

4
5
6

"I'd like to be 2 like you,"
Little 1 said, smiling at 2 yellow pears
that lay in a dish.
"Go away," said the pears.
"2 is company,
but 2 plus 1 is 3,
and that would be
a crowd."

So Little 1 sadly set off
and right away met
3 stuffed bears lazing in the sun.
If 3 is a crowd, thought Little 1,
3 plus 1 is 4,
and that is even more.
So he didn't bother to ask
if he'd be allowed to bask beside them.

But when he began
to feel lonely again,
Little 1 asked 4 bees
who were building a hive
if he might give them a hand.
"5 can do more than 4," he said.
But the biggest bee
buzzed so angrily
that Little 1 scurried away.

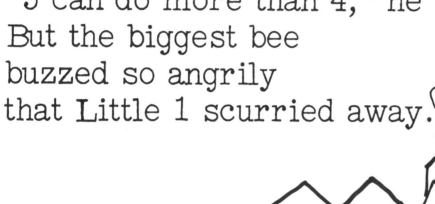

Of 5 umbrellas standing in a rack
not one answered back
when Little 1 cried,
"May I climb inside?"
But when he said,
"I'm sure there's room for 6,"
a pink parasol sniffed,
"We've no room at all
for ordinary sticks."

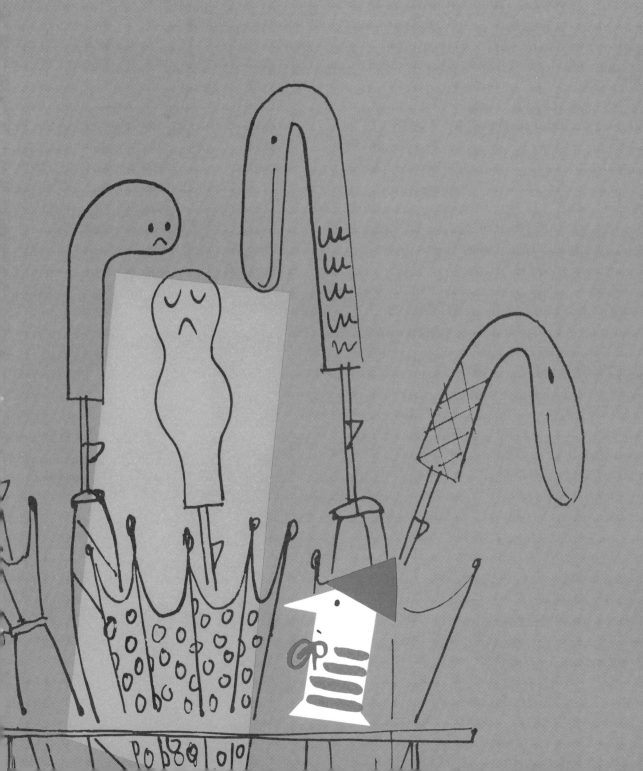

Little 1 found 6 ants
searching for crumbs of bread,
but they were too busy
to pay any attention
when Little 1 happened to mention
that instead of 6
they could as well be 7.

7 mice playing hide and seek
with a cat
just brushed Little 1 aside
when he said,
"Wouldn't it be fun
to make 8 out of 7 plus 1?"

8 stiff-backed books
on a shelf
gave 8 cross looks
when Little 1 said,
"If I stand in line,
we could then be 9."

Little 1 was in such despair
he hardly dared
to stare into a big glass bowl
and tell 9 frisky fish
it was gayer when 10 could swish.
He felt no surprise
that each fish blew a bubble
and not one took the trouble
even to reply.

Little 1 felt so alone,
he sadly started home.
"Whatever can be
the matter with me?" He sighed.
"2 turned away,
and none of the others wants to play.
Don't they know it's no fun
to be only 1?"

Little 1 was ready to cry
when a bright red hoop
came looping by.
"Hi! " cried the hoop with a smile.
"Come and play for a while. "
"But I'm only 1, " said Little 1.

"Oh no,
that's not so," cried the hoop.
"Don't you know
when a circle is empty inside
it looks like zero?
Just stand here by me,
and then we can pretend
to be number 10."

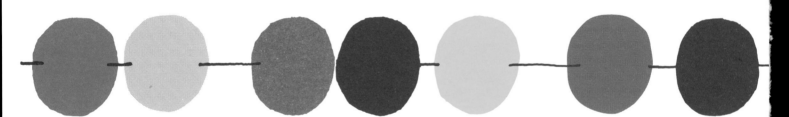

Little 1 and the hoop play together
in all kinds of places and weather.
When Little 1 pushes,
the red hoop swooshes away,
and Little 1 runs after
shouting with laughter.
Little 1 has found a friend
and has a lot of fun
now that he's no longer 1.

The 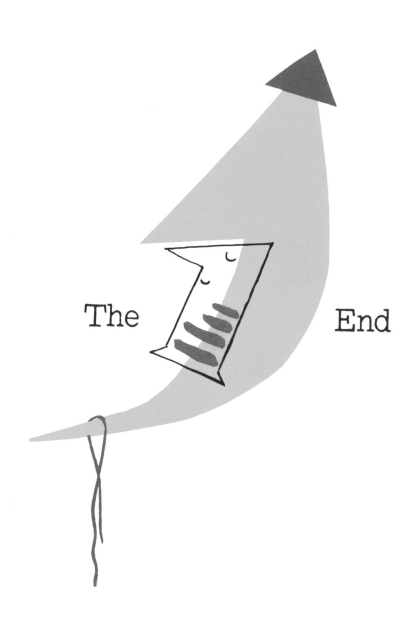 End